PUNCTUATION
Takes a Vacation

by
ROBIN PULVER

Illustrated by
LYNN ROWE REED

SCHOLASTIC INC.

New York Toronto London Auckland Sydney
Mexico City New Delhi Hong Kong Buenos Aires

ISBN 0-439-57067-0

Text copyright © 2003 by Robin Pulver.
Illustrations copyright © 2003 by Lynn Rowe Reed. All rights
reserved. Published by Scholastic Inc., 557 Broadway, New York,
NY 10012, by arrangement with Holiday House, Inc. SCHOLASTIC
and associated logos are trademarks and/or registered
trademarks of Scholastic Inc.

12 11 10 9 8 7 6 5 4   3 4 5 6 7 8/0

Printed in the U.S.A.   66

First Scholastic printing, November 2003

The text typeface is Geometric 415.

The artwork was painted with acrylics on canvas.

For Seth:
You popped the question?
Hooray!
Wishing you and Nina
a meaningful, joyful life together,
punctuated with perfect vacations.
Don't forget to send postcards!

Special thanks to Cindy Kane

R. P.

To Lael and Dan

L. R. R.

Day after day, the punctuation marks showed up in Mr. Wright's classroom.
Day after day, they did their jobs.

They put up with
being erased
and replaced
and corrected
and ignored
and moved around.

Then on the hottest, stickiest day the class had ever seen, right in the middle of a lesson about commas, Mr. Wright mopped his forehead and said, "Let's give punctuation a vacation."

yippee!

As the kids cheered and headed for the playground to cool off,

HUH?

the punctuation
marks stared
at one another
in disbelief.

"Is this the thanks we get?" asked a question mark.

"Well!" huffed an exclamation point.

"Now, now," said a comma.

out the door.

Whoosh!
They rushed back in to grab the quotation marks, who were too busy talking to pay attention.

When Mr. Wright's class returned from the playground, they couldn't wait to find out what happened in Chapter 4 of their book, *Ace Scooper, Dog Detective.*

Mr. Wright opened his mouth to read aloud, but then he stopped and stared.

THIS IS WEIRD THE PUNCTUATION IS MISSING UH OH WHERE COULD IT BE YIKES MAYBE PUNCTUATION TOOK A VACATION WE ARE IN BIG TROUBLE NOW

Mr. Wright was right. Nothing made sense without punctuation.

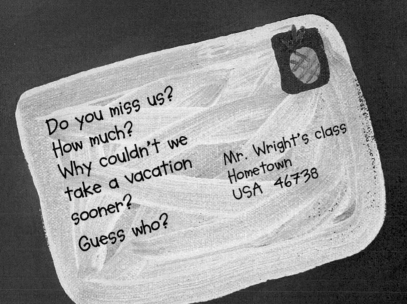

Do you miss us?
How much?
Why couldn't we
take a vacation
sooner?

Guess who?

Mr. Wright's class
Hometown
USA 46738

A couple days later,
the school secretary
delivered a small
bundle of postcards
to Mr. Wright's class.
They were postmarked
"Take-a-Break Lake."

We flop. We plop.
We stop. We stay
put in our lounge
chairs. We are
happy thinking our
complete thoughts.
Thoughtfully yours,
Sentence Stoppers

Mr. Wright's class
Hometown
USA 46738

Dear Friends,
Swimming, sailing, sunning,
soaring, waterskiing.
Next time we must
remember bug spray,
toothpaste, flashlight,
water shoes.
Sincerely,
List Makers

Mr. Wright's class
Hometown
USA 46738

Greetings to Mr. Wright's class.
This postcard doesn't take the
place of a letter. If anybody takes
the place of a letter, that's us.
It's our job. We know we're
possessive, but that's the
way we are. Don't forget
us while we're gone.

Mr. Wright's class
Hometown
USA 46738

Substitutes

The kids guessed
who wrote the postcards,
and they wanted to write back.
But they couldn't write
without punctuation.

The best they could do
was borrow some from
Mr. Rongo's class next door,
where punctuation seemed
to be running wild.

Dear, Punctuation

Please come! back We need you?
We, miss, you, too. Life at? school
is! "difficult" without, you?

We can?t do reading writing or
riddles? without punctuation
Chapter 4 of our book *Ace, Scooper,*
does,nt make sense We, will, never?
take punctuation for! granted
again. Wont you please come back
before 10 00 on Friday:

Mr Wright says. Punctuation,
please come home

Sincerely

Mr' Wright.s Class

So the punctuation marks
returned to Mr. Wright's
classroom to do the jobs
only they could do.

Mr. Rongo's unruly punctuation scrambled back to their own classroom.

Commas, periods,
exclamation points,
question marks,
colons, apostrophes,
quotation marks:
take your places.
10:00 A.M.
Time to study us.

PUNCTUATION RULES!

Quotation marks belong at the beginning and end of words a person speaks.

The **question mark** comes at the end of a question.

Use a **comma** to separate each item in a series or list. A comma also separates two complete thoughts in a sentence.

Use an **exclamation point** after a word or sentence that expresses strong feelings.

An **apostrophe** takes the place of a letter and changes two words into one word. An apostrophe is used with the letter *s* to show ownership or possession.

The **colon** lets you know what time it is. It separates the big guys (hours) from the little guys (minutes).

The **period** is the stop sign at the end of a sentence or complete thought. It is also used in abbreviations.

Punctuation marks work together to make reading and writing flow smoothly.

Mr. Wright said, "Thank you very much!" when we gave him a T-shirt from Take-a-Break Lake.

TAKE -A- BREAK LAKE

Did anybody find my missing flip-flop? Where, oh, where could it be?

That's Question Mark's flip-flop? I didn't know. It's in my suitcase.

I collected shells, stones, blisters, pinecones, feathers, and bug bites. It was fun, but I am SO tired.

Hey! Look! Great photos of us at Take-a-Break Lake!

Gosh, it's 2:15. Time to return the library book I took on vacation.

This photo is of me. I stopped two sentences from crashing into each other at the corner of Bay St. and Lake Ave.